Essentials

ABSOLUTE

ALL INSTRUMENTS

of

I0212684

Music

Theory

Don J. MacLean

Text editing by: Jeneane McKenzie

National Library of Canada Cataloguing in Publication

MacLean, Don J., 1968-
  Absolute essentials of music theory / Don J. MacLean ; Jeneane McKenzie, editor.

Includes index.
ISBN 1-896595-12-X

  1. Music theory--Elementary works. I. McKenzie, Jeneane, 1968- II. Title.
MT7.M159 2003   781   C2003-910371-4

Quantity discounts are available on bulk purchases of this book for educational purposes. For information please contact Agogic Publishing 406-109 Tenth Street, New Westminster, British Columbia, V3M 3X7, tel. (604) 290-2692, fax (604) 540-4419.

Visit us on our website:
www.GuitarAccelerator.com

Contents

About the Author

Don J. MacLean is an active freelance guitarist, composer and educator. His musical training includes studies at the Royal Conservatory of Music, Humber College, and York University, where he obtained his B.A. (Dbl. Hons. Maj.) in music and psychology. His twenty years of teaching, performing and composing have made Don a highly sought-after expert for workshops, seminars and master classes.

Don J. MacLean is the author of:

The World of Scales: A Compendium of Scales for the Modern Guitar Player
The World of Scales: A Compendium of Scales for all Instruments

Guitar Essentials: Chord Master
Guitar Essentials: Chord Master Expanded Edition
Guitar Essentials: Scale Master 1
Guitar Essentials: Scale Master Expanded Edition
Guitar Essentials: Improviser

Music Essentials: Improviser

Absolute Essentials of Music Theory
Absolute Essentials of Guitar

Guitar Quick Start

Fit Fingers Book 1
Fit Fingers Book 2

Quick Tips for Faster Fingers
Quick Tips: Guitar Technique 101
Quick Tips: Basic Guitar Chords 101
Quick Tips: Basic Guitar Scales 101

Mega Chops: Mozart for Pick-Style Guitar
Mega Chops: Bach for Pick-Style Guitar
Mega Chops: Corelli for Pick-Style Guitar
Mega Chops: Vivaldi for Pick-Style Guitar

How to Use This Book

It is best to work your way through each chapter of this book in sequential order. Each chapter builds upon the information presented in earlier chapters. The only exception to this is chapter 6 "Rhythm", which may be consulted at any time. At the end of each chapter you will find questions that will test your new found knowledge. The answers to these questions are found in the Appendix.

Chapter 1

Basics

Properties of Sound

Musical notes, although they may be produced by different instruments, all produce the same result—a series of increases and decreases in air pressure. These vibrations are picked up by our ear drums (tympanic membranes) and are transmitted to areas of the brain where we process sound. The result is the music we hear. **Pitch** refers to the relative highness or lowness of a note. **Frequency**, the number of vibrations per second, is measured in units called **Hertz** (Hz). One Hertz is equal to one vibration per second. As frequency increases so does pitch—the highest note on an acoustic piano is 4186 Hz and the lowest is 27.5 Hz.

Music Notation

Music notation is used to indicate both the pitch and duration of a note. Notes are written on a set of parallel lines called a **staff**. The vertical position of a note on the staff indicates its pitch.

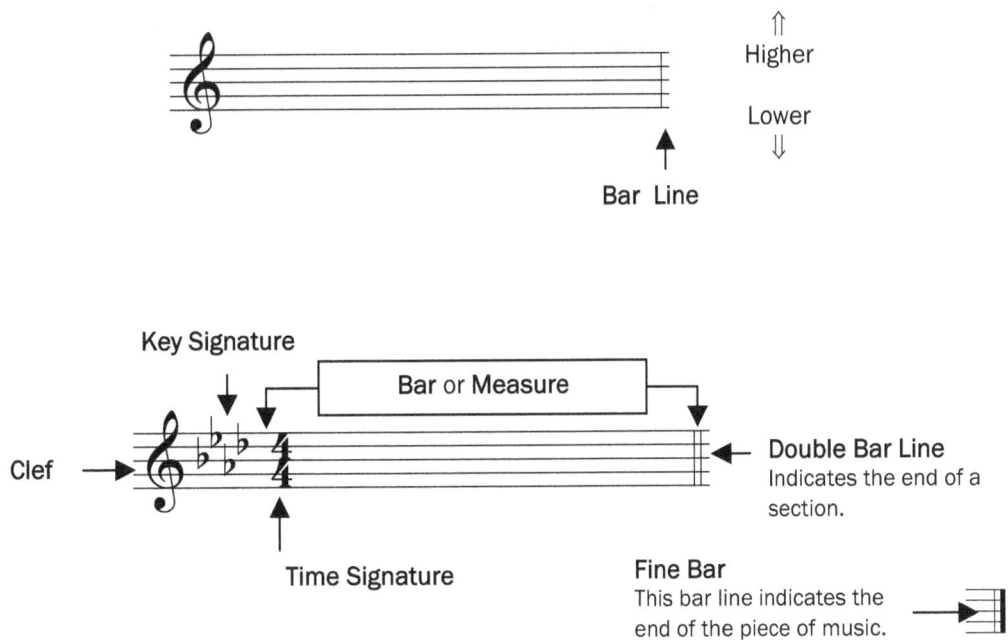

⇑
Higher

Lower
⇓

Bar Line

Key Signature

Bar or Measure

Double Bar Line
Indicates the end of a section.

Clef →

Time Signature

Fine Bar
This bar line indicates the end of the piece of music.

The first symbol you encounter in printed music is called a clef. A **clef** is a symbol used to indicate the pitch of a particular line. Once you know the pitch of one note you can easily derive the others. The musical alphabet consists of the first seven letters of the alphabet: A–B–C–D–E–F–G.

The **treble clef** is sometimes called the "G" clef because it indicates the position of the note G. An easy way to remember the notes in the treble clef is to use the following mnemonics:

Every Good Boy Deserves Fudge (notes on lines)

FACE (notes in spaces)

Treble
Clef
↓

G

F
D
B
G
E

E
C
A
F

The **bass clef** is also called the "F" clef because it indicates the position of the note F. An easy way to remember the notes in the bass clef is to use the following mnemonics:

Good Boys Deserve Fudge Always (notes on lines)

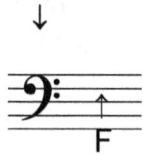

All Cows Eat Grass (notes in spaces)

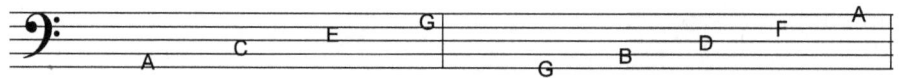

Bass
Clef
↓

F

G
E
C
A

A
F
D
B
G

To write notes that are found below or above the staff, ledger lines are used. A **ledger line** is simply an extension of the staff.

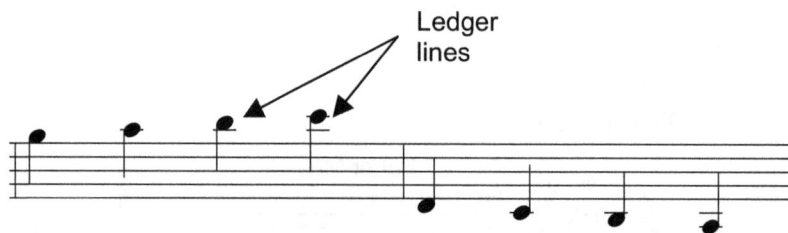

Ledger
lines

C D E F G A B C D E F G A B C

Absolute Essentials of Music Theory

When stems are added to notes, it is important that they are written in the correct direction. Notes above the middle line usually have their stems all written down. Notes that are below the middle line should have their stems written in an upwards direction. A note found on the middle line can have its stem go in either direction.

When notes are joined, the stems will take the direction of the note that is the greatest distance from the middle line of the staff.

UNDERSTANDING SHARPS (♯) AND FLATS (♭)

The smallest standard distance between any two given notes in the West, is the semitone. The semitone can be found between any two adjacent keys on the piano. In other words, take any key on the piano and go to the note immediately above or below it. The whole tone is the distance of two semitones.

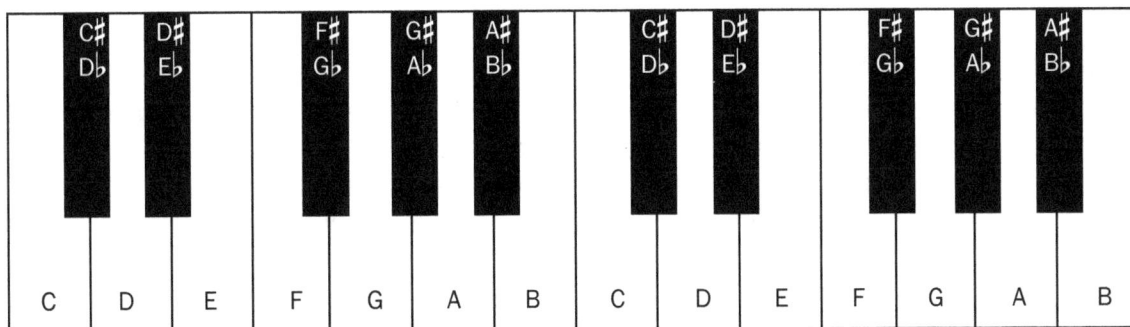

A sharp (♯) raises a note by one semitone.

A flat (♭) lowers a note by one semitone.

A natural (♮) cancels the previous sharp or flat and returns the note to its original pitch.

A double sharp (x) raises a natural note by two semitones.

A double sharp (**x**) raises a sharp by one semitone
.
A double flat (♭♭) lowers a natural note by two semitones.

A double flat (♭♭) lowers a flat by one semitone.

- If you raise a **natural note** (♮) by one semitone, the note will become a sharp. A natural note is a note that is not sharp or flat.
- If you lower a natural note one semitone, it will become a flat.
- By raising a flat (♭) one semitone, you obtain a natural note.
- Lowering a sharp (♯) one semitone, will give you a natural note.

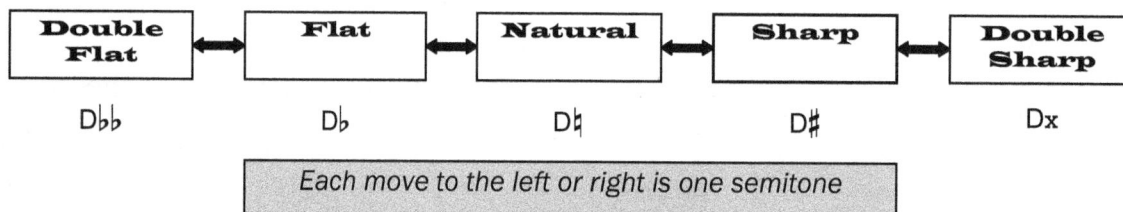

Double Flat		Flat		Natural		Sharp		Double Sharp
D♭♭	↔	D♭	↔	D♮	↔	D♯	↔	Dx

> Each move to the left or right is one semitone

For example:
- If you raise an F one semitone, it becomes an F♯.
- If you raise a D♭ one semitone, it becomes a D♮.
- If you lower a G one semitone, it becomes a G♭.
- If you lower a G♯ one semitone, it becomes a G♮.
- If you lower an A♭ one semitone, it becomes an A♭♭.
- If you raise a G♯ one semitone, it becomes a Gx.

Enharmonic Equivalents

Enharmonic equivalents are notes that sound the same but are written with different letter-names. For example, the F♯ and G♭ both sound identical on the piano. G♯ and A♭ also share the same black key on the piano. Context determines whether a note should be called an F♯ or a G♭. Here are some other notes you should know about:

B♯ = C   E♯ = F   F♭ = E   C♭ = B

When you see a sharp or flat between the treble clef and the time signature, the sharp(s) or flat(s) effect the music from that point forward. The collection of sharps or flats is called a **key signature**. In the following example, all of the F's are sharp. The F♯ found in the key signature effects all F♯'s regardless of octave. A more detailed discussion is found in chapter 2.

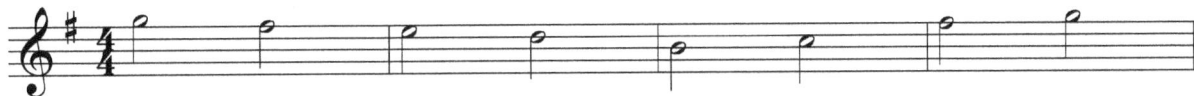

Sharps or flats that are not part of the key signature (called **accidentals**) effect only the measure in which they appear. The next bar line cancels out all previous sharps or flats that are not part of the key signature. A natural sign cancels accidentals for the remainder of the measure.

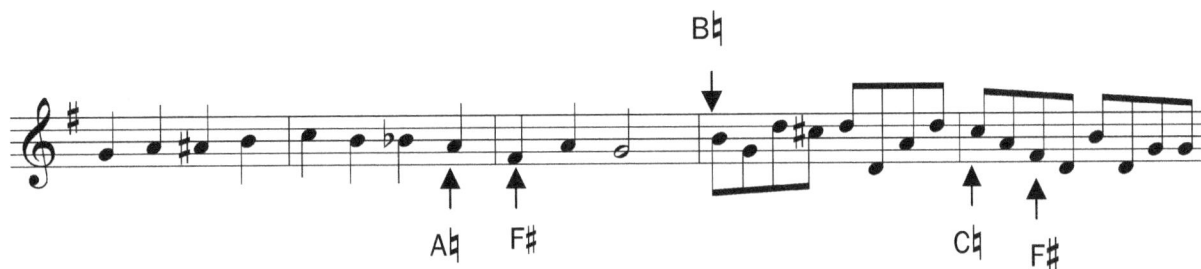

Exercises

1. Identify the following notes.

2. Write enharmonic equivalents for the following notes:

a) E♭
b) G♯
c) F♯
d) B♯
e) C♭
f) F♭
g) A♯

3. Semitones and whole tones.

a) If you raise a G♭ one semitone you have _____
b) If you raise a B one whole tone you have _____
c) If you raise an A one semitone you have _____
d) If you raise a C♯ one whole tone you have _____
e) If you lower a G♭ one semitone you have _____
f) If you lower an F one whole tone you have _____
g) If you lower a D♭ one semitone you have _____

Absolute Essentials of Music Theory

Chapter 2

Scales

What are Scales?

The word scale comes from the Italian word *scala*, which means ladder. A **scale** is a collection of pitches that have been arranged into a specific ascending and descending order. Scales are used as a basis for composition or as a vehicle for improvisation.

The Major Scale

The *major scale* is often used for the derivation of many of the theoretical principles of Western music theory and also happens to be the most common scale in popular music. Consequently, this will be the first scale to be examined.

In order to have a *major scale*, there must be a specific arrangement of semitones and whole tones. The C major scale consists of the following notes:

C   D   E   F   G   A   B   C

T = **Whole Tone:** A whole tone is the distance of two semitones. The whole tone is also called a *tone* or a *whole step*.

ST = **Semitone:** The semitone is also known as a *half step*.

C (T) D (T) E (ST) F (T) G (T) A (T) B (ST) C

To build any major scale simply proceed through the following progression of semitones and whole tones:

Major Scale Formula:-   T T ST T T T ST

If you follow this formula starting with any note other than C, you will find that you are required to use sharps or flats. Here is a list of all of the major scales.

C major	C D E F G A B C
G major	G A B C D E F♯ G
D major	D E F♯ G A B C♯ D
A major	A B C♯ D E F♯ G♯ A
E major	E F♯ G♯ A B C♯ D♯ E
B major	B C♯ D♯ E F♯ G♯ A♯ B
F♯ major	F♯ G♯ A♯ B C♯ D♯ E♯ F♯
C♯ major	C♯ D♯ E♯ F♯ G♯ A♯ B♯ C♯

F major	F G A B♭ C D E F
Bb major	B♭ C D E♭ F G A B♭
Eb major	E♭ F G A♭ B♭ C D E♭
Ab major	A♭ B♭ C D♭ E♭ F G A♭
Db major	D♭ E♭ F G♭ A♭ B♭ C D♭
Gb major	G♭ A♭ B♭ C♭ D♭ E♭ F G♭
Cb major	C♭ D♭ E♭ F♭ G♭ A♭ B♭ C♭

Key Signatures

Sharps and flats are written on the staff in a specific order and are collectively called a **key signature**. This standardization means that when you see one sharp, you will be in the key of G major and the one sharp, will be the F♯. If you see three flats, you would be in the key of E♭. The exceptions to this will be discussed later.

There are a total of 15 major scales. However, of these 15 scales, only 12 actually sound different. When you were introduced to the sharps and flats in Chapter 1, you were introduced to the concept of **enharmonic equivalents**. The C♭ major scale sounds identical to the B major scale; the G♭ major scale sounds the same as the F♯ major scale; and the D♭ major scale has the same sound as the C♯ major scale. Context will determine the most appropriate scale choice. If a composition is in the key of B major and **modulates** (changes keys) to F♯ major, it would be most logical to write the composition in F♯ major instead of G♭ major. The reason is quite simple, moving from B to F♯ major would mean moving from five to six sharps. If you were to go from B to G♭, you would have to cancel out the five sharps in the B major scale and introduce 6 flats. There are other theoretical reasons why you would favor one key over the other on paper, but they do not concern us here.

The easiest way to learn the notes in each major scale is to memorize the following:

C major	No sharps or flats
G major	One sharp
D major	Two sharps
A major	Three sharps
E major	Four sharps
B major	Five sharps
F♯ major	Six sharps
C♯ major	Seven sharps
F major	One flat
B♭ major	Two flats
E♭ major	Three flats
A♭ major	Four flats
D♭ major	Five flats
G♭ major	Six flats
C♭ major	Seven flats

Take note of the number of sharps or flats contained in each scale. A great way to memorize the major scales is to first memorize:

C major has no sharps or flats;
C♯ major has every note sharp; and
C♭ major has every note flat.

Now take the remaining scales and pair them up. Take each pair of scales, and spend a little time each day repeating the number of sharps or flats that occur in the scale. It is best to recite the notes in each scale ascending and descending. For example, on day one, you would repeat that G major has one sharp (F♯) and D major has two sharps (F♯ and C♯). The notes in each of these ascending and descending scales are:

G major: G A B C D E F♯ G; G F♯ E D C B A G

D major: D E F♯ G A B C♯ D; D C♯ B A G F♯ E D

Repeat the notes in the scales throughout the day. On the next day, you would memorize that A major has three sharps and E major has four sharps. You should also repeat all of the scales you learnt over the previous day(s). Do this with the remaining scales and you will learn all of the major scales and their notes in just six days.

On the following page, you will find a mnemonic that will help you learn the sharps and flats. The first letter of each word represents the note(s) that is/are sharp in the key. G major has one sharp and the one sharp is F♯ (Father). D major has two sharps and the sharps are F♯ and C♯ (Father Charles). B major has five sharps: F♯, C♯, G♯, D♯ and A♯ (Father Charles Goes Down And). As you can see, the sharps are cumulative when presented in the order shown.

Sharps
Father Charles Goes Down And Ends Battle

In all key signatures, you will find each note that is to be sharp or flat, is indicated only once on the staff. For example, in A major there are three sharps, F♯, C♯ and G♯. On the staff, you will notice that these sharps are only indicated in one octave. When a note is marked as sharp or flat by a key signature, it means that all like notes are sharp or flat as well. The following example demonstrates this concept.

All of the F's, C's and G's are sharp in A major:

Unless a song changes keys, the key signature found at the beginning of a piece of music indicates that the entire piece of music is in a certain key. A change of key, or **modulation** as it is more formally known, would be indicated by introducing a new key signature.

To memorize the order that flats appear in a key signature you can reuse the mnemonic device introduced for the sharps. For the flats, it is simply read backwards:

Flats
Battle Ends And Down Goes Charles Father

B♭ major has two flats: B♭ and E♭ (**B**attle **E**nds). A♭ major has four flats: B♭, E♭, A♭ and D♭ (**B**attle **E**nds **A**nd **D**own).

Minor Scales

Minor scales are used in most styles of music and are second in popularity to the major scale. Minor scales do not have their own unique key signatures but borrow from what is referred to as their **relative major scale**. To build a minor scale, go to the VI degree of the major scale and re-write the scale (including any sharps or flats) commencing on this sixth note. Roman numerals are often used to notate scale degrees.

C major

C	D	E	F	G	A	B	C
					⇑		
					VI		

A minor

A	B	C	D	E	F	G	A

Table of Natural Minor Scales

A minor:	A B C D E F G A
E minor:	E F♯ G A B C D E
B minor:	B C♯ D E F♯ G A B
F♯ minor:	F♯ G♯ A B C♯ D E F♯
C♯ minor:	C♯ D♯ E F♯ G♯ A B C♯
G♯ minor:	G♯ A♯ B C♯ D♯ E F♯ G♯
D♯ minor:	D♯ E♯ F♯ G♯ A♯ B C♯ D♯
A♯ minor:	A♯ B♯ C♯ D♯ E♯ F♯ G♯ A♯
D minor:	D E F G A B♭ C D
G minor:	G A B♭ C D E♭ F G
C minor:	C D E♭ F G A♭ B♭ C
F minor:	F G A♭ B♭ C D♭ E♭ F
B♭ minor:	B♭ C D♭ E♭ F G♭ A♭ B♭
E♭ minor:	E♭ F G♭ A♭ B♭ C♭ D♭ E♭
A♭ minor:	A♭ B♭ C♭ D♭ E♭ F♭ G♭ A♭

Natural Minor

Table of Relative Minor Scales

C major	C D E F G A B C
A minor	A B C D E F G A
G major	G A B C D E F♯ G
E minor	E F♯ G A B C D E
D major	D E F♯ G A B C♯ D
B minor	B C♯ D E F♯ G A B
A major	A B C♯ D E F♯ G♯ A
F♯ minor	F♯ G♯ A B C♯ D E F♯
E major	E F♯ G♯ A B C♯ D♯ E
C♯ minor	C♯ D♯ E F♯ G♯ A B C♯
B major	B C♯ D♯ E F♯ G♯ A♯ B
G♯ minor	G♯ A♯ B C♯ D♯ E F♯ G♯

F♯ major	F♯ G♯ A♯ B C♯ D♯ E♯ F♯
D♯ minor	D♯ E♯ F♯ G♯ A♯ B C♯ D♯
C♯ major	C♯ D♯ E♯ F♯ G♯ A♯ B♯ C♯
A♯ minor	A♯ B♯ C♯ D♯ E♯ F♯ G♯ A♯
F major	F G A B♭ C D E F
D minor	D E F G A B♭ C D
B♭ major	B♭ C D E♭ F G A B♭
G minor	G A B♭ C D E♭ F G
E♭ major	E♭ F G A♭ B♭ C D E♭
C minor	C D E♭ F G A♭ B♭ C
A♭ major	A♭ B♭ C D♭ E♭ F G A♭
F minor	F G A♭ B♭ C D♭ E♭ F
D♭ major	D♭ E♭ F G♭ A♭ B♭ C D♭
B♭ minor	B♭ C D♭ E♭ F G♭ A♭ B♭
G♭ major	G♭ A♭ B♭ C♭ D♭ E♭ F G♭
E♭ minor	E♭ F G♭ A♭ B♭ C♭ D♭ E♭
C♭ major	C♭ D♭ E♭ F♭ G♭ A♭ B♭ C♭
A♭ minor	A♭ B♭ C♭ D♭ E♭ F♭ G♭ A♭

Below you will see the key signatures for each minor scale.

Am   Em   Bm   F♯m   C♯m   G♯m   D♯m   A♯m

Am   Dm   Gm   Cm   Fm   B♭m   E♭m   A♭m

Harmonic Minor Scale

To build a **harmonic minor scale**, raise the VII degree of the minor scale.

A minor:

A   B   C   D   E   F   G   A
⇑
VII

A harmonic minor:

A   B   C   D   E   F   G♯   A
⇑
VII

Harmonic Minor

Absolute Essentials of Music Theory

A Harmonic Minor   D Harmonic Minor   G Harmonic Minor   C Harmonic Minor

F Harmonic Minor   B♭ Harmonic Minor   E♭ Harmonic Minor   A♭ Harmonic Minor

Melodic Minor Scale

To build a **melodic minor scale,** raise the VI and VII degrees of the minor scale ascending and lower them descending.

A melodic minor ascending (raise VI & VII):
A   B   C   D   E   F♯   G♯   A

⇑   ⇑

VI   VII

A melodic minor descending (lower VI & VII):
A   G♮   F♮   E   D   C   B   A

⇑   ⇑

VII   VI

The melodic minor scale has a different ascending and descending form. The descending form is the same as the natural minor scale. For the purpose of improvisation, the ascending version will yield the most interesting possibilities. This ascending form is very common in jazz improvisation. When the melodic minor scale's ascending form (raised VI and VII) is used ascending and descending, you have what is referred to as the *Jazz Minor* or the *Real Melodic Minor scale.*

A Jazz Minor:
A   B   C   D   E   F♯   G♯   A

You may also find it helpful to think of the Jazz Minor scale as being a major scale with a ♭3.

Melodic Minor

Absolute Essentials of Music Theory

Pentatonic Scales

A pentatonic scale is a five note scale. There are many different types of pentatonic scales, but the most common are the major and minor pentatonic scales.

The major pentatonic scale is quite often derived by omitting the IV and VII degrees of the major scale. For example, to build a C major pentatonic scale you would drop the F and B from the C major scale.

C major:

C	D	E	F	G	A	B	C
			⇑			⇑	
			IV			VII	

C major pentatonic:

C   D   E   G   A   C

The same procedure is often followed for the derivation of the minor pentatonic scale except this time the II and VI degrees are dropped from the minor scale:

A minor:

A	B	C	D	E	F	G	A
	⇑				⇑		
	II				VI		

A minor pentatonic:

A   C   D   E   G   A

Major Pentatonic

C major pentatonic   G major pentatonic   D major pentatonic   A major pentatonic

E major pentatonic   B major pentatonic   F♯ major pentatonic   C♯ major pentatonic

C major pentatonic   F major pentatonic   B♭ major pentatonic   E♭ major pentatonic

A♭ major pentatonic   D♭ major pentatonic   G♭ major pentatonic   C♭ major pentatonic

Minor Pentatonic

A minor pentatonic   E minor pentatonic   B minor pentatonic   F♯ minor pentatonic

C♯ minor pentatonic   G♯ minor pentatonic   D♯ minor pentatonic   A♯ minor pentatonic

A minor pentatonic   D minor pentatonic   G minor pentatonic   C minor pentatonic

F minor pentatonic   B♭ minor pentatonic   E♭ minor pentatonic   A♭ minor pentatonic

Absolute Essentials of Music Theory

Exercises

1. Using letter-names, write the notes for the following scales:

   a) A major
   b) E minor
   c) G harmonic minor
   d) F♯ major
   e) D♭ major
   f) G melodic minor
   g) B pentatonic minor

2. In the treble clef, write the following scales with the appropriate key signatures.

   a) E major
   b) A♭ major
   c) C♯ harmonic minor
   d) F melodic minor
   e) F minor pentatonic
   f) G melodic minor

3. What is the relative minor or major scale for the following:

   a) G major
   b) D minor
   c) F♯ minor
   d) F♯ major

Chapter 3

Intervals

Intervals

An **interval** is the distance between any two given notes. Notes that are played simultaneously are called **harmonic intervals**, while notes that are played one after the other, are referred to as **melodic intervals**.

To determine the size of an interval, simply count from the lower note to the upper note of the interval. When counting up, remember to count the starting note as one. For example, to determine the distance between the notes F and E, you would arrive at the distance of a seventh.

F	G	A	B	C	D	E
1	2	3	4	5	6	7

After determining the distance between the two notes, you must next determine the interval's **quality**. You now compare the upper note to the major scale of the lower note. If the upper note is contained in the major scale of the lower note (i.e., if the E is contained in the F major scale in the above example), you have a **diatonic interval**.

The diatonic intervals of a major scale are: the *perfect unison, major second, major third, perfect fourth, perfect fifth, major sixth, major seventh* and the *perfect octave.*

perfect unison | major 2nd | major 3rd | perfect 4th | perfect 5th | major 6th | major 7th | perfect octave

Interval Classification

The unison, fourth, fifth and the octave (8th) are considered to be *perfect intervals*. If a perfect interval is raised by one semitone, it becomes an *augmented interval*. A perfect interval lowered by one semitone will become a *diminished interval*.

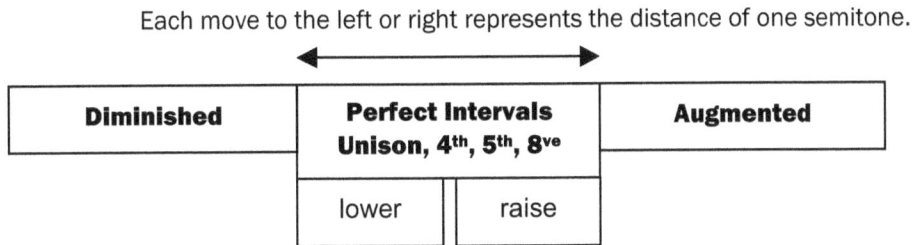

Each move to the left or right represents the distance of one semitone.

Diminished	Perfect Intervals Unison, 4th, 5th, 8ve	Augmented
	lower | raise	

The remaining intervals, the second, third, sixth and the seventh, are considered to be *major* intervals, if the upper note of the interval is contained in the major scale of the lower note. A major interval that is lowered by one semitone, becomes a *minor* interval. A lowered minor interval, becomes a *diminished* interval. If a major interval is raised, it will be called an *augmented* interval.

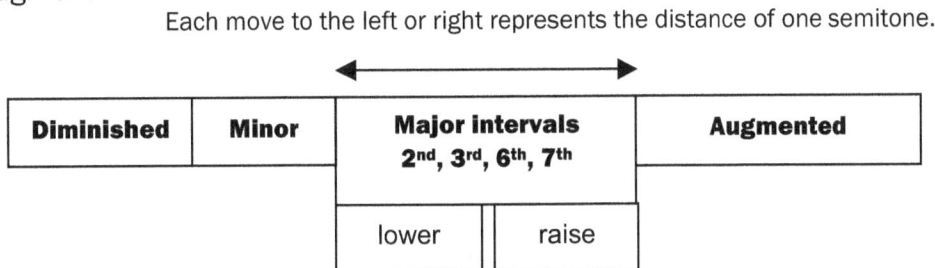

Each move to the left or right represents the distance of one semitone.

Diminished	Minor	Major intervals 2nd, 3rd, 6th, 7th	Augmented
		lower | raise	

The preceding discussion of intervals dealt with **simple intervals**. A simple interval is an interval that is no larger than an octave. Any interval that is larger than an octave is deemed to be a **compound interval**. The most common compound intervals are the ninth, eleventh and thirteenth.

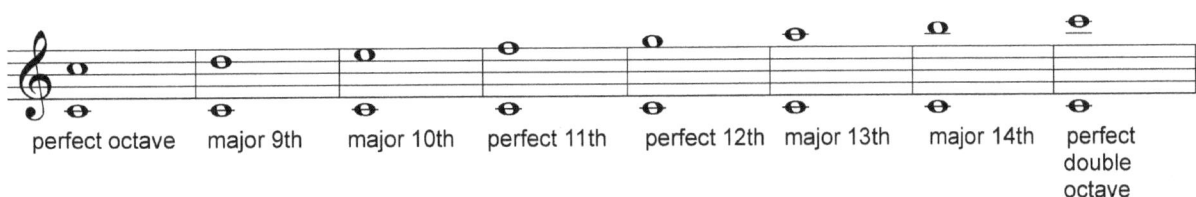

1 2 3 4 5 6 7 8 9 10 11 12 13 14 15

perfect octave | major 9th | major 10th | perfect 11th | perfect 12th | major 13th | major 14th | perfect double octave

Compound intervals take on the same quality as their simple interval counterparts. A major second above C is the note D. A major 9th above C is also a D.

| ma 2 | ma 9 | ma 3 | ma 10 | P4 | P11 | P5 | P12 | ma 6 | ma 13 | ma7 | ma 14 | perfect octave | perfect double octave |

Just as you can have an aug 2nd, min 2nd, or a dim 2nd, you can therefore have an aug 9th, min 9th, or a dim 9th.

Maj. 2nd   Aug. 2nd   Min. 2nd   Dim. 2nd   Maj. 9th   Aug. 9th   Min. 9th   Dim 9th

You can also have enharmonic intervals. The most common enharmonic equivalent intervals are:

aug 4 ⇔ dim 5
aug 2 ⇔ min 3
aug 6 ⇔ min 7
dim 7 ⇔ maj 6

Inverting Intervals

Simple intervals can be inverted. Inversion can be accomplished by either moving the bottom note of the interval up an octave, or by moving the top note of the interval down an octave.

When an interval is inverted you will find:

Perfect intervals remain **perfect**
Major intervals become **minor**
Minor intervals become **major**
Augmented intervals become **diminished**
Diminished intervals become **augmented**

To solve inverted intervals you can either count the actual distance between the notes, or you can subtract the interval from 9.

P unison   P8   P5   P4   P4   P5   ma 2   mi 7

9 - 1=8   9 – 5 =4   9 – 4 =5   9 – 2 =7

ma 3   mi 6   ma 6   mi 3   ma 7   mi 2   mi 2   ma 7

mi 3   ma 6   mi 6   ma 3   mi 7   ma 2   aug 2   dim 7

aug 5   dim 4   aug 4   dim 5

Exercises

1. Identify the following intervals:

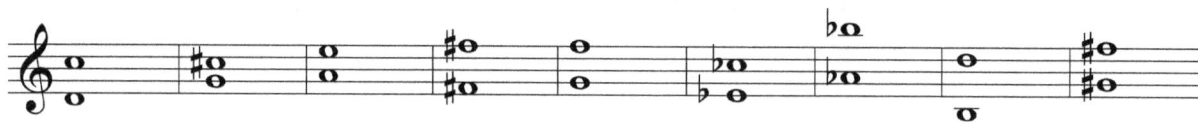

2. Identify the following intervals then invert and solve on the staff below.

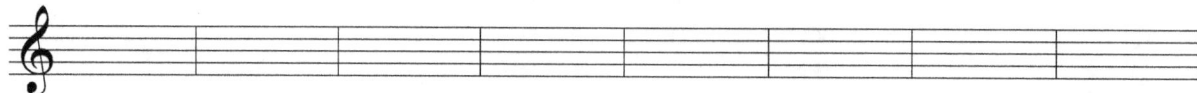

Musical staff with empty measures

Chapter 4

Chords

A chord is three or more notes played simultaneously. Chords provide accompaniment and support for melodies. There are many different types of chords, but the most common are called triads.

Triads

A **triad** is a chord that contains three different notes. To understand how chords are built, we must return to the major scale. Take the first, third and fifth notes from the C major scale and you will have a C major chord.

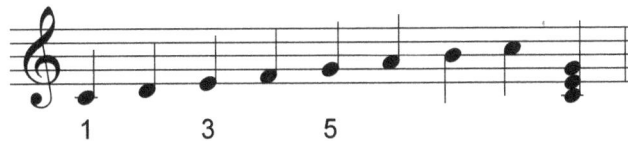

Here is how to build any chord:
1) Look at the appropriate formula for the chord you want.
2) Go to the major scale of the chord. It does not matter whether you want a D♭ major triad or a D♭ diminished chord, you would still go to the D♭ major scale and extract the appropriate notes.
3) Extract the necessary notes from the formula.
4) Alter any necessary notes to fit the formula.

The flat (♭) symbol means to lower a note by a semitone while the sharp (♯) symbol indicates that the note must be raised by one semitone. As you extract the notes from the major scale be sure to remember the notes that are sharp or flat. If a note is already sharp in the major scale and must be lowered to follow a chord formula, it will become a natural note (♮). The figure below denotes the possible alterations.

Double Flat (♭♭)	Flat (♭)	Natural (♮)		Sharp (♯)	Double Sharp (x)
		lower	raise		
D♭♭	D♭	D		D♯	Dx

(Each move to the left or right represents the distance of a semitone.)

Major	1 3 5
Minor	1 ♭3 5
Diminished	1 ♭3 ♭5
Augmented	1 3 ♯5
Suspended 4	1 4 5
Suspended 2	1 2 5

Example 1. G major: Formula $\Rightarrow$ 1 3 5

Take the first, third and fifth notes out of the G major scale.

G major:

G	A	B	C	D	E	F♯	G
1	2	3	4	5	6	7	8
⇑		⇑		⇑			

For a major chord, you simply extract the first, third and fifth notes from the major scale. Therefore the notes in a G major chord are:

G	B	D
1	3	5

Example 2. D minor: Formula $\Rightarrow$ 1 ♭3 5

Take the first, third and fifth notes out of the D major scale.

D major:

D	E	F♯	G	A	B	C♯	D
1	2	3	4	5	6	7	8
⇑		⇑		⇑			

For a minor chord, you must lower the third. The F♯ will become an F♮. Therefore the notes in a D minor chord are:

$$\begin{array}{ccc} \text{D} & \text{F}♮ & \text{A} \\ 1 & ♭3 & 5 \end{array}$$

Example 3. A♭ diminished: Formula ⇒ 1 ♭3 ♭5

Take the first, third and fifth notes out of the A♭ major scale.

A♭ major:

$$\begin{array}{cccccccc} \text{A}♭ & \text{B}♭ & \text{C} & \text{D}♭ & \text{E}♭ & \text{F} & \text{G} & \text{A}♭ \\ 1 & 2 & 3 & 4 & 5 & 6 & 7 & 8 \\ ⇑ & & ⇑ & & ⇑ & & & \end{array}$$

For a diminished chord, you must lower the third and fifth notes from the major scale. The C will become an C♭ and the E♭ will become an E♭♭. Therefore the notes in an A♭ diminished chord are:

$$\begin{array}{ccc} \text{A}♭ & \text{C}♭ & \text{E}♭♭ \\ 1 & ♭3 & ♭5 \end{array}$$

Example 4. F♯ augmented: Formula ⇒ 1 3 ♯5

Take the first, third and fifth notes out of the F♯ major scale.

F♯ major:

$$\begin{array}{cccccccc} \text{F}♯ & \text{G}♯ & \text{A}♯ & \text{B} & \text{C}♯ & \text{D}♯ & \text{E}♯ & \text{F}♯ \\ 1 & 2 & 3 & 4 & 5 & 6 & 7 & 8 \\ ⇑ & & ⇑ & & ⇑ & & & \end{array}$$

For an augmented chord, extract the first, third and fifth notes from the major scale and raise the 5th by one semitone. The C♯ will become a Cx. Therefore the notes in an F♯ augmented chord are:

$$\begin{array}{ccc} \text{F\#} & \text{A\#} & \text{Cx} \\ 1 & 3 & \text{\#5} \end{array}$$

Example 5. F suspended 4: Formula ⇒ 1 4 5

Take the first, fourth and fifth notes out of the F major scale.

F major:

$$\begin{array}{cccccccc} \text{F} & \text{G} & \text{A} & \text{B}\flat & \text{C} & \text{D} & \text{E} & \text{F} \\ 1 & 2 & 3 & 4 & 5 & 6 & 7 & 8 \\ \Uparrow & & & \Uparrow & \Uparrow & & & \end{array}$$

For a suspended 4 chord, you simply extract the first, fourth and fifth notes from the major scale. Therefore the notes in an F sus 4 chord are:

$$\begin{array}{ccc} \text{F} & \text{B}\flat & \text{C} \\ 1 & 4 & 5 \end{array}$$

Example 6. A♭ suspended 2: Formula ⇒ 1 2 5

Take the first, second and fifth notes out of an A♭ major scale.

A♭ major:

$$\begin{array}{cccccccc} \text{A}\flat & \text{B}\flat & \text{C} & \text{D}\flat & \text{E}\flat & \text{F} & \text{G} & \text{A}\flat \\ 1 & 2 & 3 & 4 & 5 & 6 & 7 & 8 \\ \Uparrow & \Uparrow & & & \Uparrow & & & \end{array}$$

For a suspended 2 chord, extract the first, second and fifth notes from the major scale. Therefore the notes in an A♭ sus 2 chord are:

$$\begin{array}{ccc} \text{A}\flat & \text{B}\flat & \text{E}\flat \\ 1 & 2 & 5 \end{array}$$

Just as there is no standardization of scale names from one region to another, there are many problems with the current system of identifying chords. The following abbreviations are frequently used:

maj $\Rightarrow$ for major

min $\Rightarrow$ for minor

dim $\Rightarrow$ for diminished

aug $\Rightarrow$ for augmented

sus 4 $\Rightarrow$ for suspended 4

sus 2 $\Rightarrow$ for suspended 2

Often the major chord will have no indication following its letter-name. For example, the chords C maj, F maj and G maj, may be written as C, F, G. Minor chords are often abbreviated with a lowercase "m", "mi", "min", or a minus sign "–". The diminished triad is sometimes symbolized as a min ♭5, or as dim (triad). Bear in mind that "dim" is sometimes used to represent a diminished 7th chord. The augmented chord, which is usually abbreviated as "aug", is sometimes symbolized with a plus sign (+). For example, G+ and A♭+, would both be augmented triads. You should note that the plus sign is used to represent the major chord in some texts that cover classical music theory. Below you will see a summary of the most common ways that basic triads are symbolized.

Triad	Common Symbols	Best
Major	C, C ma, C Maj, C maj, C major, C Major, C+	C, C ma, C maj, C Maj
Minor	C mi, C min, C minor, C-, C m,	C mi, C min
Diminished	C dim, C°, C (dim), C min ♭5, C° (no 7), C° (omit 7)	C min ♭5, C dim, C dim(triad)
Augmented	C+, C aug, C aug 5, C ♯5, C +5	C aug, C+

Triad Inversions

For variety and to allow for the smooth transition from one chord to the next, you will sometimes encounter inversions. In an inversion, either the third or the fifth of the chord is the lowest sounding note of the chord.

Major

C major	C/E	C/G	C major

Root position	1st inversion	2nd inversion	root position

In root position the root (1) of the chord is the bass note. First inversion has the third in the bass and second inversion has the fifth in the bass. In modern notation you will see inversions notated as chord/bass note. For example, C/E means that you play a C major chord with E in the bass. A D/F♯ would mean that you play a D major chord and have F♯ as the lowest pitched note.

The most common triad inversions involve the standard triads: major, minor, diminished and augmented. The sus chords are not usually inverted, but when they are, their notation can become quite cumbersome.

Minor

C minor	C min/E♭	C min/G	C min

Root position	1st inversion	2nd inversion	root position

Diminished

C diminished	C dim/E♭	C dim/G♭	C dim

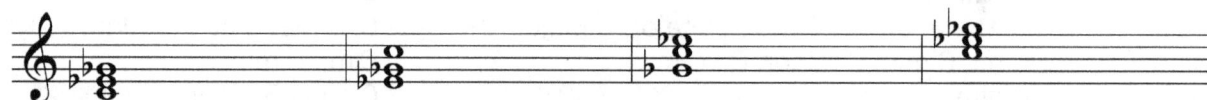

Root position	1st inversion	2nd inversion	root position

Augmented

C augmented	C aug/E	C aug/G♯	C aug

Root position	1st inversion	2nd inversion	root position

Triad Identification

To identify a triad, you must first place the triad in root position. Chords are often written in **open position**—spread out over a distance greater than an octave. As you will recall, chords are built by stacking consecutive thirds (sus chords are an exception to this). This means that you should be able to write out the notes of a chord so that they appear on consecutive lines or spaces of the staff. When you have the notes written on consecutive lines or spaces of the staff, you have arranged the chord into **close position**. You can now determine the quality and inversion of the chord.

Absolute Essentials of Music Theory

B♭/D   B♭   A♭/E♭   A♭   F min/A♭   F min   E/G♯   E

In the first measure above, you find the notes D-B♭-F. If you rearrange these notes so that they fall on consecutive lines or spaces, you end up with the B♭ major chord shown in measure 2. Therefore, the chord in measure 1 is a B♭ major chord with a D in the bass, i.e., 1st inversion. Follow the same procedure and you can solve for the rest of the chords above.

Doubling

As you can see in the chords shown below, notes may be doubled. This has no effect on naming a chord, but does somewhat alter the sound of the chord. It is important to note that no matter how spread out a chord is, it is always the lowest note that determines a chord's position. Doubling or even tripling chord tones is done to create a "bigger" sound or for smooth voice-leading. Voice-leading is the practice of connecting the notes from one chord to the next chord in a smooth fashion. This is covered in the study of harmony and counterpoint.

C   C   F/C   F

Exercises

1. Identify the following chords:

2. In the treble clef notate the following chords:

    a) D min
    b) A dim
    c) B♭
    d) C aug
    e) G sus 2
    f) F♯
    g) A♭ dim
    h) B sus 4

3. Re-write the following chords in close position on the staff below and identify the chord quality and position of both chords.

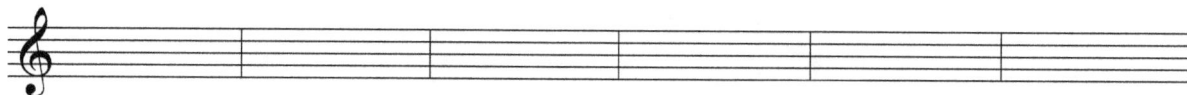

Chapter 5

Harmonized Scales

Chords can be built on each note of a scale. For example, if you were to write out a C major scale and build chords off of each degree, your result would be a harmonized major scale:

Diatonic Triads

C	Dmin	Emin	F	G	Amin	Bdim	C

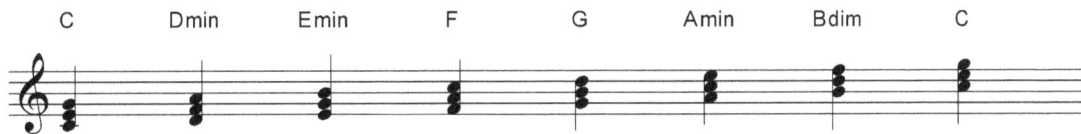

To build chords on each degree of a scale you first write out the scale:

Now simply stack thirds on top of each scale degree:

Solving Triads

Here is how to determine the type of chord that is found on each note the major scale.

Step 1 Take the bottom note of the chord and compare the other notes of the chord to the major scale of the bottom note.

Step 2 Now compare the intervals to the triad formulas presented in chapter 4.

> Take the bottom note of the chord and compare the chord tones to the major scale of this note. The bottom note in this example is a C, so you would compare the notes C-E-G to see if these notes are contained in the C major scale. Since they are contained in the C major scale, we know that they have not been altered in any way. The notes C-E-G are 1-3-5 in the key of C. The formula for a major triad is 1-3-5. Therefore this would be a C major triad.

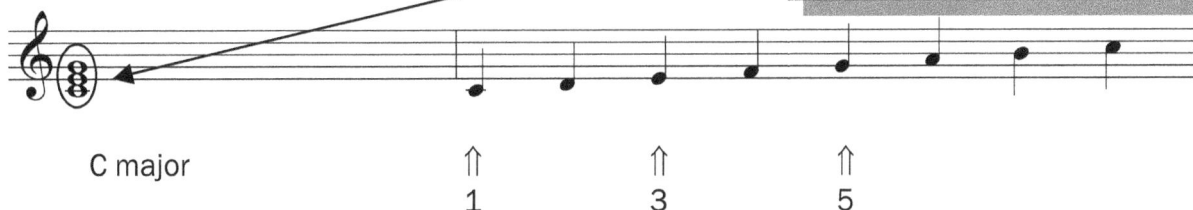

C major   1   3   5

D major key signature

Notes in comparison to C major.

D minor
1   ♭3   5

For this chord the notes are D-F-A. If we look at the notes in the D major scale (D-E-F♯-G-A-B-C♯), we see that the F and C are both sharp. The notes in the chord are D-F-A. Therefore, the F has been lowered by one semitone. We end up with 1-♭3-5, forming a D minor chord. Remember that the chords we are examining here are built off of each note of the C major scale. The C major scale has no sharps or flats.

E minor
1   ♭3   5

Now compare the notes E-G-B to the E major scale (E-F♯-G♯-A-B-C♯-D♯). Here we see that the G should be sharp to form an E major triad. The third has been lowered by a semitone so the result is, E min: E-G-B, 1-♭3-5.

F major
1   3   5

The notes F-A-C form an F major triad.

G major
1   3   5

The G major triad consists of the notes G-B-D.

A minor
1   ♭3   5

In A major the notes are A-B-C♯-D-E-F♯-G♯-A. An A major chord would therefore consist of A-C♯-E. The notes in this chord are A-C-E, meaning that the third has been lowered by one semitone. The result is 1-♭3-5, A-C-E, an A minor chord.

Absolute Essentials of Music Theory

B dim

⇑   ⇑   ⇑
1   ♭3   ♭5

The notes in B major are: B-C♯-D♯-E-F♯-G♯-A♯-B. The VII chord in C major consists of the notes B-D-F. If this was a B maj triad it would contain B-D♯-F♯. Since we have B-D-F, it means that each note has been lowered by one semitone. If you consult the formulas in chapter 4 you will see that the 1-♭3-♭5 constitutes a diminished triad.

Examine the chords below:

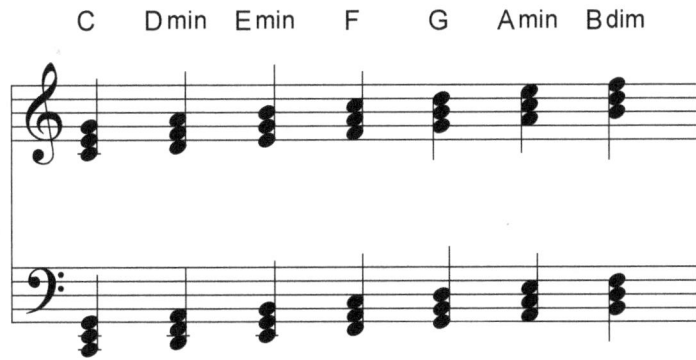

C   D min E min   F   G   A min B dim

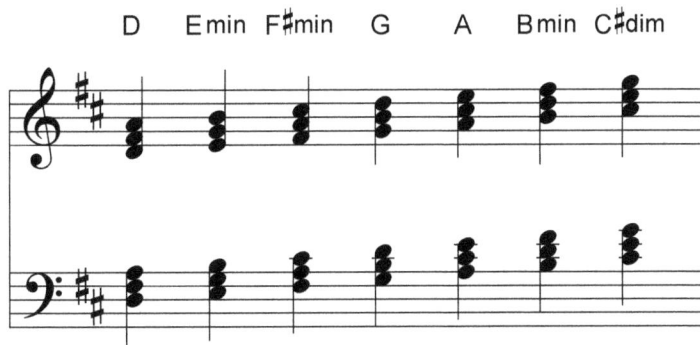

D E min F♯min G   A B min C♯dim

Notice that the chords built on the first, fourth and fifth degrees are all major chords. The chords built on the second, third and sixth degrees are minor and the chord built on the seventh note of the scale is diminished. This is a consistent pattern encountered in all major scales.

I	Major
II	Minor
III	Minor
IV	Major
V	Major
VI	Minor
VII	Diminished

Using this pattern, you can quickly determine the chords in any major scale. Let's say you need to know the chords found in E major. The notes in E major are E-F#-G#-A-B-C#-D#-E. Using the above formula our result is:

I	E major
II	F# minor
III	G# minor
IV	A major
V	B major
VI	C# minor
VII	D# diminished

E   F#min G#min   A   B   C#min D#dim

Here are all of the triads in every major scale:

Harmonized Major Scales

C   Dmin   Emin   F   G   Amin   Bdim   C

I   II   III   IV   V   VI   VII   I

G   Amin   Bmin   C   D   Emin   F#dim   G

D   Emin   F#min   G   A   Bmin   C#dim   D

A   Bmin   C#min   D   E   F#min   G#dim   A

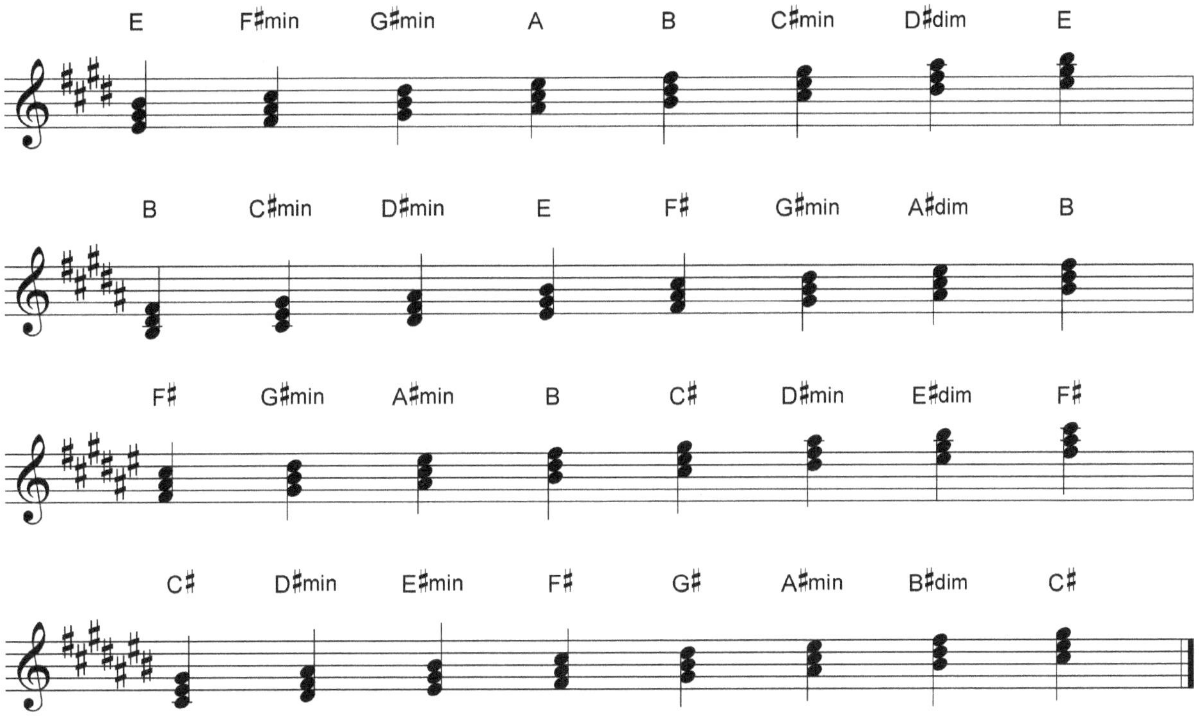

Harmonized Major Scales

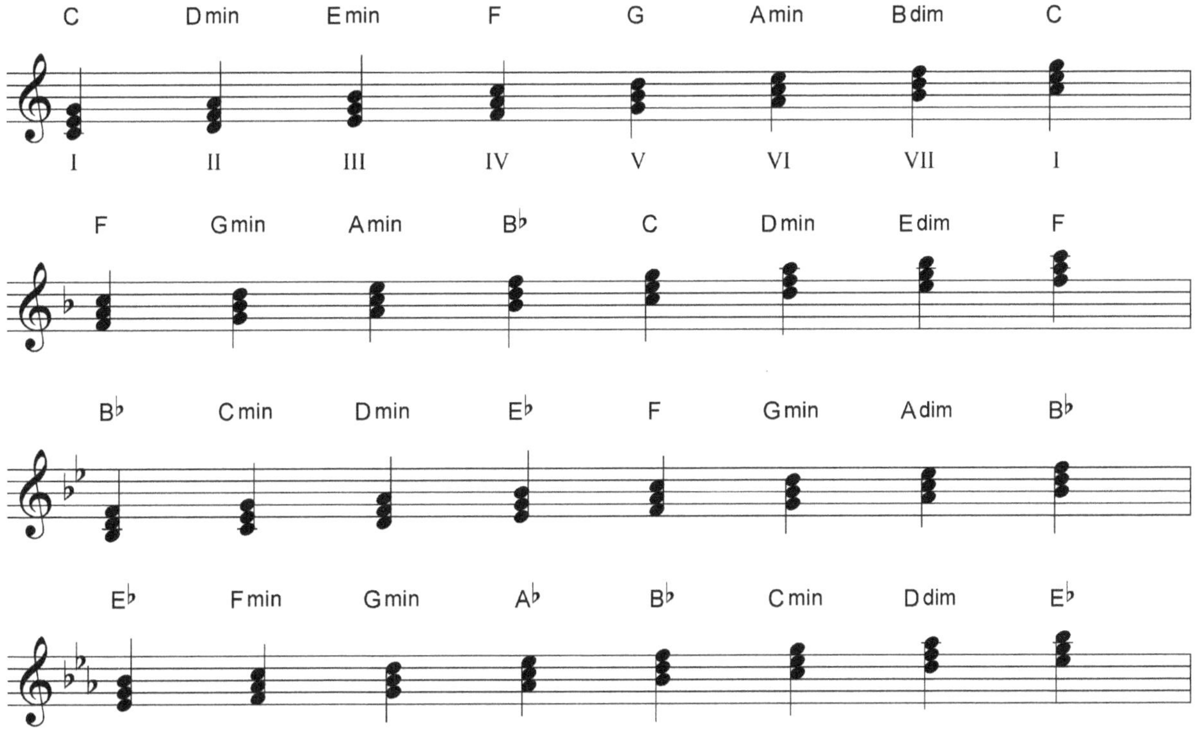

You can also build triads on each degree of the minor, harmonic minor and melodic minor scales.

Natural Minor Triads

The triads in minor also follow a pattern. The following is true in all minor keys:

I	Min
II	Dim
III	Maj
IV	Min
V	Min
VI	Maj
VII	Maj

Absolute Essentials of Music Theory

Harmonic Minor Triads

In harmonic minor the following is true:

I	Min
II	Dim
III	Aug
IV	Min
V	Maj
VI	Maj
VII	Dim

Jazz Minor Triads

In jazz minor the following is true:

I	Min
II	Min
III	Aug
IV	Maj
V	Maj
VI	Dim
VII	Dim

Harmonized Natural Minor Scales

Absolute Essentials of Music Theory

Harmonized Natural Minor Scales

Harmonized Harmonic Minor Scales

Harmonized Harmonic Minor Scales

Harmonized Jazz Minor Scales

Absolute Essentials of Music Theory

Harmonized Jazz Minor Scales

Exercises

1.   Identify the following chords:

      a) What is the II chord in A major   _____

      b) What is the I chord in A♭ major   _____

      c) What is the V chord in B major   _____

      d) What is the III chord in F major   _____

      e) What is the II chord in D♭ major   _____

      f)   What is the VI chord in C♯ major   _____

      g) What is the II chord in G major   _____

      h) What is the VII chord in A major   _____

      i)   What is the IV chord in E major   _____

      j)   What is the V chord in D major   _____

      k) What is the III chord in F♯ major   _____

      l)   What is the III chord in F♯ minor   _____

      m) What is the I chord in F♯ harm min _____

      n) What is the VII chord in D minor   _____

      o) What is the V chord in G jazz min   _____

      p) What is the IV chord in E harm min _____

2.   In the treble clef write all of the triads in:

      a) G major

      b) F major

      c) B♭ major

      d) D min

      e) B major

      f)   C harmonic minor

      g) F jazz minor

Chapter 6

Rhythm

Levels of Rhythmic Activity

Music is usually organized in a repeatable accent pattern known as meter. In free time, music unfolds with an unpredictable accent pattern (i.e. there are no recurring accents). If a performer plays a note, then several others quickly, then pauses for a while and plays additional notes, you would have an example of free time. This means that there is no time signature being used. If we were to notate this example with vertical slashes, here is what we would have:

```
    >              >
    I         III I I                      I II
```

The vertical slashes represent the notes and the distance between each slash represents time. The accent symbol (>) indicates the notes that are emphasized or accented.

Pulse/Beat

You will occasionally encounter music where each beat is an equal distance apart, but the accent pattern does not appear to repeat. In this instance you have music that has an unpredictable occurrence of strong and weak beats. Strong beats are very definite, while weak beats are of a more subtle nature.

S   W   S   S   S   W   W   S   W etc.

S = strong
W = weak

Meter

When you have a recurring repeatable accent pattern, you have meter. The repeatable accent pattern will consist of a combination of strong and weak beats. For example:

2/4 time consists of:
    S   W

3/4 time consists of:
    S   W   W

4/4 time consists of:
    S   W   M   W (M stands for medium weak)

5/4 time consists of:
    S   W   S   W   W
or
    S   W   W   S   W

S W M W | S W W | S W S W W or: S W W S W

Time Values

The most common time signature, 4/4, (pronounced four-four) is often abbreviated with a fancy "C" and called common time. In 4/4, the whole note receives four beats or counts. The half note receives two beats and the quarter note receives one beat. Eighth notes each receive half of a beat.

or

Note Durations

Note Durations

Whole note	Half notes	Quarter notes	Eighth notes

Count:
1 2 3 4   1   2   3   4   1   2   3   4   1 + 2 + 3 + 4 +

Eighth notes are sometimes written without connecting beams:

The whole note receives 4 beats; the half note receives 2 beats; a quarter note receives 1 beat and an eighth note receives 1/2 of a beat; a sixteenth note receives 1/4 of a beat and the triplet receives 1/3 of a beat.

Sixteenth notes   Triplets

1 e & ah 2 e & ah 3 e & ah 4 e & ah   1 & ah 2 & ah 3 & ah 4 & ah

Rest Durations

Rest Durations

Whole note rest   Half note rests   Quarter note rests   Eighth note rests

Count:
1 2 3 4   1 2 3 4   1 2 3 4   1 + 2 + 3 + 4 +

Sixteenth note rests

1 e + ah 2 e + ah 3 e + ah 4 e + ah

Time Signatures

A time signature is used to indicate the strong and weak beats in a measure and also which note value receives one beat. In **Simple Time** (2/2, 2/4, 2/8, 3/2, 3/4, 3/8, 4/2, 4/4, 4/8), the top number of the time signature indicates the number of beats per measure while the bottom number indicates the type of note that receives one beat. For example:

2/4
Two beats per measure
Quarter note receives one beat

3/4
Three beats per measure
Quarter note receives one beat

4/4
Four beats per measure
Quarter note receives one beat

In Simple Time you tap your foot on each beat. In **Compound Time**, (6/4, 6/8, 6/16, 9/4, 9/8, 9/16, 12/4, 12/8, 12/16) you should tap your foot on each major beat division. In 6/8 time the measure is divided into two (1 2 3), (4 5 6). Nine-eight time has three main divisions (1 2 3), (4 5 6), (7 8 9). Twelve-eight time is comprised of 4 main divisions (1 2 3), (4 5 6), (7 8 9), (10 11 12). In 6/8 you would count 1 2 3 4 5 6, but only tap your foot on 1 and 4. In 9/8 you would count 1 2 3 4 5 6 7 8 9, and tap your foot on 1, 4, and 7. In 12/8 time you count 1 2 3 4 5 6 7 8 9 10 11 12, and tap your foot on 1, 4, 7, and 10.

Dotted and Tied Notes

Ties and dots are used to increase the time value of the notes they follow. A **dot** increases the time value of a note by half. A half note receives 2 beats; a dotted half note receives 3 beats. A quarter note receives one beat; a dotted quarter note receives one and a half beats. An eighth note receives half of a beat; a dotted eighth note receives half of a beat plus one quarter of a beat (in other words 3/4's of a beat).

Absolute Essentials of Music Theory

The notes in a tie are of the same pitch. A **tie** increases the time value of a note by the value of the second note. You do not sound the second note of the tie. You simply sustain the note for the duration of the first note plus the value of note it is tied to.

Repeats
Instead of writing out the same music twice, repeats are used.

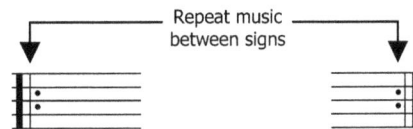

Repeat music between signs

First and Second Endings
To perform first and second endings, the passage is repeated but the ending is different the second time.

Exercises

1.   Add time signatures for the following examples:

Conclusion

Congratulations! You now know the absolute essentials of music theory. The concepts covered in this book, should be applied to your instrument and to the analysis of the music you listen to and play. In addition, you should create your own questions for the concepts covered in this book. For example:

- Using letter-names, write all of the major scales that contain one or more flat.
- Using letter-names, write all of the major scales that contain one or more sharp.
- What major scale contains two sharps?
- What major scale contains five sharps?
- What natural minor scale contains no flats?
- What natural minor scale contains six sharps?
- What natural minor scale contains four flats?
- Using letter-names, write a B harmonic minor scale.
- Using letter-names, write an F♯ harmonic minor scale.
- Using letter-names, write a D melodic minor scale.
- Using letter-names, write a D jazz minor scale.
- What is the relative minor of G major?
- What is the relative major of G minor?
- What is the relative minor of D major?
- What is the relative minor of E♭ major?
- What are the notes of in a D minor chord?
- What notes make up a G major chord?

You can also work on your understanding of music when you are away from your instrument. Work on mental drills when you don't have your instrument handy. For example, ask yourself: "What major scale contains five flats?" "What are the notes in a B♭ major scale?" "What notes are found in a D diminished triad?" Practice reciting the notes in scales ascending and descending. Name all of the triads contained in each major scale, etc. Using this "down time" to mentally practice theory, will enable you to master theory and will allow you to devote most of your practice time to actually playing your instrument.

Appendix

Answers

Chapter 1   Basics

1.

B B G Bb G G F Gb C C G D# Gb D# A

A F# B E B D E D# C E D E A A# D

A D C G C B D B D A B# Bb C F Bb

In the first measure above, the third last note is a Gb not a G. This is because a Gb was introduced earlier in the measure. Remember that accidentals effect any additional occurrences of the note in the measure. The bar line cancels out accidentals.

2. Write enharmonic equivalents for the following notes:

a) Eb ⇔ D#

b) G# ⇔ Ab

c) F# ⇔ Gb

d) B# ⇔ C

e) Cb ⇔ B

f) Fb ⇔ E

g) A# ⇔ Bb

3. Semitones and whole tones.

a)   If you raise a G♭ one semitone you have _____ G♮

b)   If you raise a B one whole tone you have _____ C♯/D♭

c)   If you raise an A one semitone you have _____ A♯/B♭

d)   If you raise a C♯ one whole tone you have _____ D♯/E♭

e)   If you lower a G♭ one semitone you have _____ G♭♭/F

f)   If you lower an F one whole tone you have _____ E♭/D♯

g)   If you lower a D♭ one semitone you have _____ C/D♭♭

For each of the above answers enharmonic equivalents are shown. Context will determine what the "correct" answer is. You will understand this after completing the chapters on intervals and chords.

Chapter 2   Scales

1. Using letter-names, write the notes for the following scales:

a) A major
    A B C♯ D E F♯ G♯

b) E minor
    E F♯ G A B C D

c) G harmonic minor
    G A B♭ C D E♭ F♯

d) F♯ major
    F♯ G♯ A♯ B C♯ D♯ E♯

e) D♭ major
    D♭ E♭ F G♭ A♭ B♭ C

f) G melodic minor
    G A B♭ C D E♮ F♯ G F♮ E♭ D C B♭ A G

g) B pentatonic minor
    B D E F♯ A

2. In the treble clef, write the following scales with the appropriate key signatures.

E major

Ab major

Ab major pentatonic

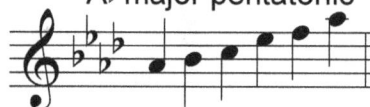

C# Harmonic Minor

F Melodic Minor

F minor pentatonic

G Melodic Minor

3. What is the relative minor or major scale for the following:
    a) G major ⇔ E minor
    b) D minor ⇔ F major
    c) F♯ minor ⇔ A major
    d) F♯ major ⇔ D♯ minor

Chapter 3   Intervals

1.

min 7   aug 4   P5   P8   min 7   min 6   maj 9   min 10   min 7

The G♯ to F♯ interval found in the last measure of question 1 is a bit tricky. To solve intervals, you have been told to go to the major scale of the bottom note of the interval. If you review over the major scales found in chapter 2, you will find that there is no listing for G♯ major. Here is how you can solve this interval:

The notes in a G major scale are:

G major

G A B C D E F♯ G

Therefore to derive the notes in G♯, you simply raise every note in the G major scale by one semitone. The result is:

G♯ major

G♯ A♯ B♯ C♯ D♯ E♯ Fx G♯

Now that we have the G♯ major scale you can see that the F would have to be an Fx to be a major seventh. The interval is therefore a minor 7th.

2.

maj 3   P5   maj 2   aug 7   aug 4   P5   maj 6   aug 5

min 6   P4   min 7   dim 2   dim 5   P4   min 3   dim 4

Chapter 4   Triads

1.

C   Fdim   E♭min   A   A♭min   Gdim   Fsus2   Esus4

Faug   C♯sus2   F♯min   Fsus4   A♯min   Baug   Daug

2.

Dmin   Adim   B♭   Caug   Gsus2   F♯   A♭dim   Bsus4

3.

F   A/E   Fmin   Gaug/B   B♭dim/D♭   E♭/G

F   A   Fmin   Gaug   B♭dim   E♭

Absolute Essentials of Music Theory

Chapter 5   Harmonized Scales

1.   Identify the following chords:
   a) What is the II chord in A major   _____B min
   b) What is the I chord in A♭ major   _____A♭
   c) What is the V chord in B major   _____F♯
   d) What is the III chord in F major   _____A min
   e) What is the II chord in D♭ major   _____E♭ min
   f) What is the VI chord in C♯ major   _____A♯ min
   g) What is the II chord in G major   _____A min
   h) What is the VII chord in A major   _____G♯ dim
   i) What is the IV chord in E major   _____A
   j) What is the V chord in D major   _____A
   k) What is the III chord in F♯ major   _____A♯ min
   l) What is the III chord in F♯ minor   _____A
   m) What is the I chord in F♯ harm min   _____F♯ min
   n) What is the VII chord in D minor   _____C
   o) What is the V chord in G jazz min   _____D
   p) What is the IV chord in E harm min   _____A min

2.   In the treble clef, write all of the triads in:
   a) G major

   b) F major

   c) B♭ major

d) D min

| D min | E dim | F | G min | A min | B♭ | C | D min |

e) B major

| B | C#min | D#min | E | F# | G#min | A#dim | B |

f) C harmonic minor

| C min | D dim | E♭aug | F min | G | A♭ | B dim | C min |

g) F jazz minor

| F min | G min | A♭aug | B♭ | C | D dim | E dim | F min |

1.

Index

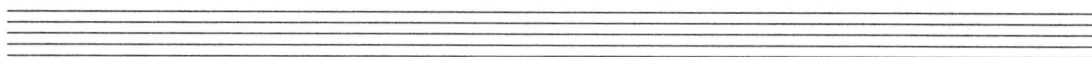

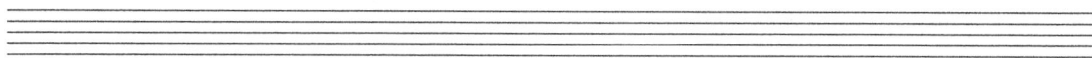

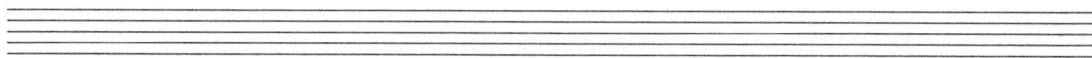

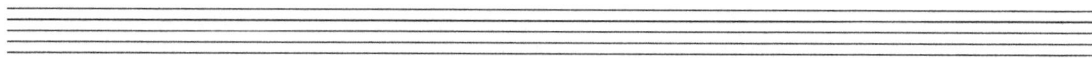

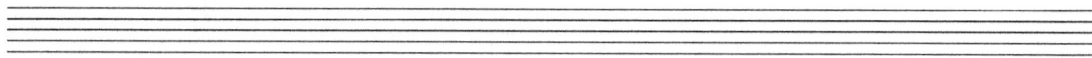

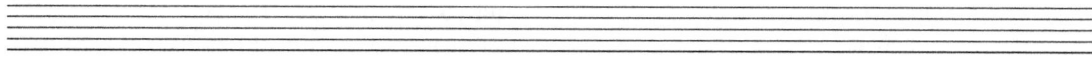

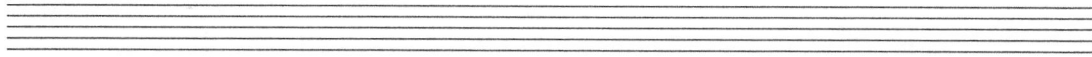

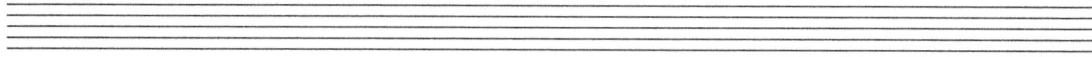

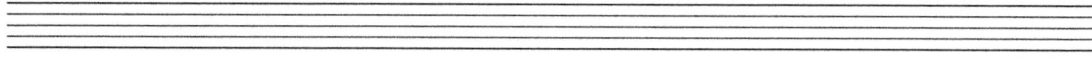

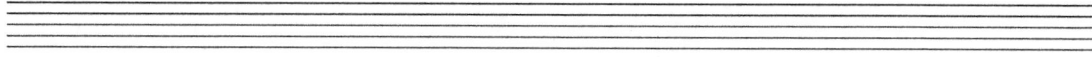

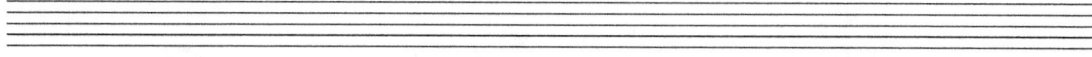

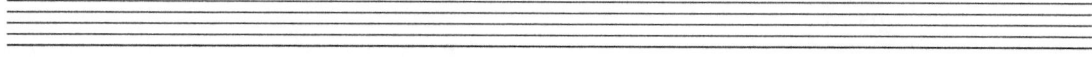

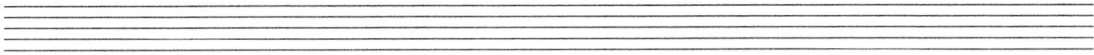

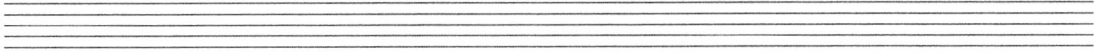

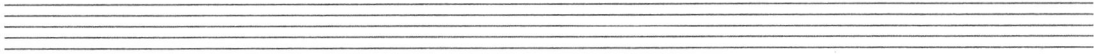

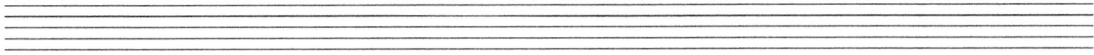

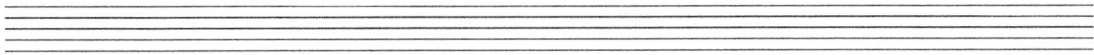

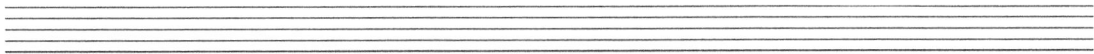

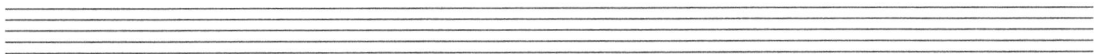

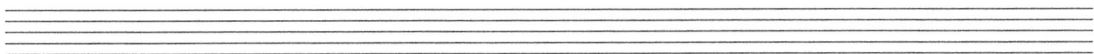

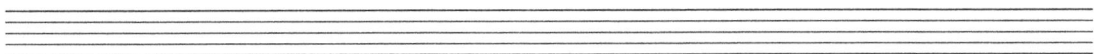

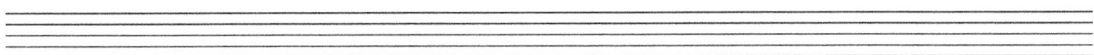

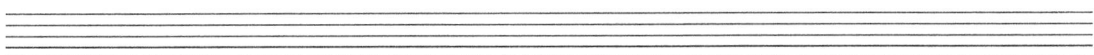

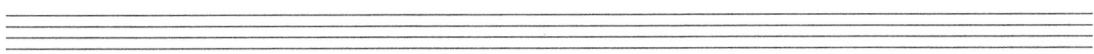

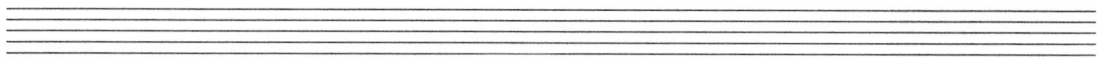

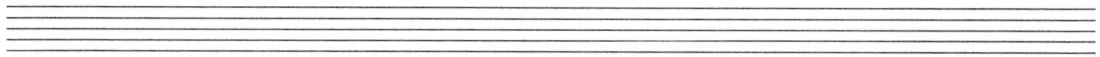

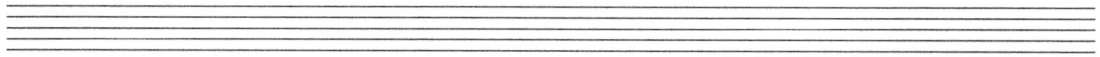

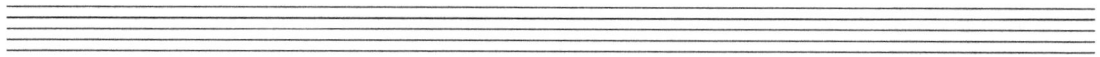

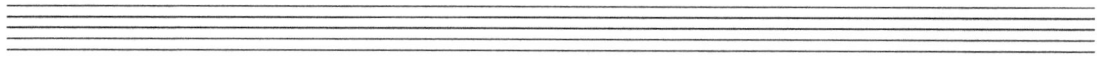

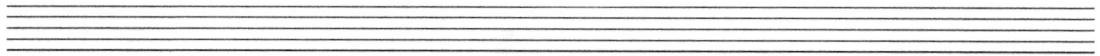

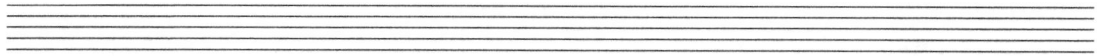

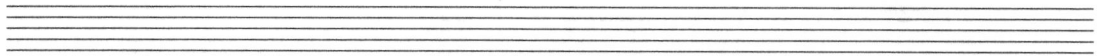

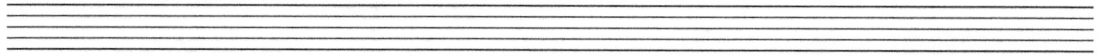

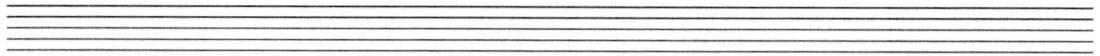

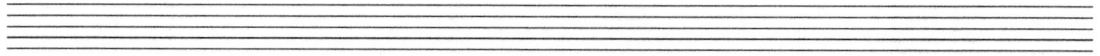

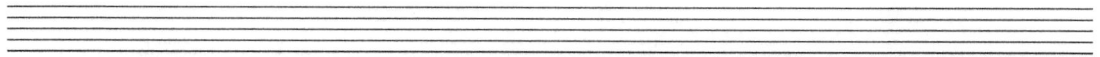